THIS WORKBOOK BELONGS TO:

DEDICATION

To all of my clients past, present, and future who are determined, motivated, and relentless in the pursuit of their own happiness and authenticity. May you find the courage you seek to be truly you. Much love.

ABOUT THIS WORKBOOK

This is a 31 day journey into becoming who you already are. Who you are on a deep, cellular level and on a deeper, soul level. That person that you WANT to be is already inside of you but maybe you haven't accepted her into your heart yet. No matter who you are, think you are, were, want to be, think you want to be, this workbook is here to help you gain clarity on your life purpose, path, and identity. I am honored and excited for what lies ahead.

DISCLAIMER

All information and resources found in this book are based on the opinions and experimentation of the author, Danna Yahav. All information is intended to motivate and inspire readers to make their own health care and mental health decisions after consulting with their healthcare provider. Danna Yahav is not a doctor, lawyer, psychiatrist, or therapist. No part of this book shall be interpreted as a diagnosis for any medical condition. The information in this book is not intended to replace a relationship with a qualified health care professional and is not intended as medical advice.

TABLE OF CONTENTS

"I have been a seeker and still am.
But I stopped asking the books and the stars.
I started listening to the teaching of my soul."
-Rumi

INTRO

Welcome, soul sister.

This book was born from my own hunger to find my true self, lose my old self, and re-create myself. It has been a journey. One that continues to evolve and never really ends. But it does get more fun. Who I am today may not be who I am tomorrow and that's ok. As humans we are always changing and growing. If you are not growing you are dying. So allow yourself to change as often as you feel necessary. Never stop exploring your inner depths, your shadows, your gifs, your desires, and your light. This is your purpose.

My intention for you with this workbook is that it may help you find your path again. That you may have the opportunity to feel into the experience of being your most authentic self. That you may learn new things about yourself, that you may accept your flaws and strengths, and that you may love yourself regardless. And finally I pray that you may find the hope and inspiration to be, do, and have, whatever your heart desires.

At 30 years old, going through my first Saturn Return, I found myself having everything I ever wanted yet still falling into a deep depression. I had the job, the family, the kids, the life. I was the person everyone wanted me to be. Except me.

Because you see, the soul ALWAYS knows when we are living in alignment with our truest selves and when we are not. It gives us warning signs. For the latter: depression, job loss, end of relationships, addictions, etc. There are always warning signs before we truly jump into the depths of misconception and illusion.

For me, it was addictions, job loss, and a deep feeling of disconnection. Disconnection from who I was and who I felt I should be. Disconnection from the light, the dark, God, spirit, the Universe, the Earth, myself. Everything. You name it, I was disconnected from it. Except maybe wine. Wine and I were very connected. It was a feeling of pure numbness.

Aside from the pain of not being happy with the life I had consciously created (and had previously wanted so badly) was the realization that I had no idea who I really was and what I really desired out of life. How is that possible? How could I be 30 years old and not know who I was?

I started going to therapy to try to find answers by digging in to the past (which I really had no memory of), but more on this later. I found a lot of clarity in expressing my thoughts and feelings openly. It had been a long time since I allowed myself that luxury. As many women do, I had taken on the role of the strong one, the one who had it all together, the mom that could do it all… at the sake of my wellbeing.

At the time I had been studying Eastern medicine and metaphysics for about 7 years, on and off. I tried to convince my therapist that I could heal with the help of charka clearings, mediums, psychics, and spirit work. She said that perhaps she would no longer be able to serve me because she had no experience with this sort of thing. She pointed me in the direction of local MeetUp groups where I found The Being One Center in Warminster, PA that would literally bring me back to life. I don't want to undermine my journey by telling you that I was healed or figured it all out after I started going to this center. But it was certainly an incredible start. It put the fire back in my belly. I was excited to learn and absolutely fascinated by the spirit world and my own intuitive gifts. In short, it LIT me up in a huge way.

I write this book after 3 full years, 7 coaches, 344,577 books, 25,000 hours, 43 courses/classes, past life regressions, CBD meditations, shadow work, light work, angel work, dark work, energy work, shamanic work, healers, clearers, cleansers, mediums, psychics, and so much more. So you would think that I have it all figured out by now, right? HA! I don't. But does anyone really have it ALL figured out? I do, however, feel a deep sense of connection. Connection to my true being, to my own truth, and to my real self. Kind of a slow learner right? I will totally own up to that. Historically, I need to make the same mistake at least 12 times before I actually "get it". ;) The point I am trying to make is that this stuff didn't come easy to me. It took determination, work, and focus. But the most important thing is that the PAIN of staying the same was much worse than the courage it took to do the work for a better life.

Any deep work on yourself can be difficult. But it doesn't have to take you 15 years or even 3. It all depends on your mentors, your support, and how deep you are willing to go with yourself. Super coach Rich Litvin says, "The best time to plant a tree was 20 years ago. The second best time to plant a tree is today." That's the point, just start. Start somewhere, anywhere, start now. With me.

Who am I and why should you even care what I have to say?
I am a lifelong spiritual seeker, learner, grower, follower, and leader. The difference between the me 10 years ago and the me now is that I can finally see myself, accept myself, and love myself.

I don't love labels. They are restrictive, judgmental, and are often only half truths. So as far as what I am… I am a girl. A wife. A mom. A friend. A daughter. A coach. A teacher. An empathizer. An intuitive. And I reserve the right to change my identity whenever I want!

I am a lover of spirituality, metaphysics, angels, spirits, prayer, Universal laws, synchronicities, crystals, energy, love, meditation, Quantum physics, forgiveness, and tequila.

I believe everything happens for a reason. I believe we create our lives each and every day. I believe in being in creation mode rather than just responding to life. I believe in values and having a mindset of fucking steel. I believe in therapy, self awareness, selfishness, breathing, and surrender.

I've been blessed to help many other people on this journey and THAT on it's own is worth the sleepless nights, the tears, the confusion, the hangovers, the anger, the misery, and the disconnection from truth. Because remember, I KNOW everything happens for a reason. And you are my reason. I am meant to learn, to grow, and then help. Imagine if we all shared that perspective on life.

The rest of this workbook is everything I have learned to date that I use for myself and with clients. I hope that it helps you as much as it has helped me and my clients.

Please be consistent with journaling, loving yourself, and be supportive of others for everyone is fighting their own battle.

The work here is part shadow work, part intuition development, part manifestation, part mysticism, and all magic.

Enjoy.

PS - I LOVE to seeing your posts, receiving your comments, and reading your messages! Tag me on Instagram @this.is.danna or find me in my FREE Facebook group: The Conscious Creators' Club

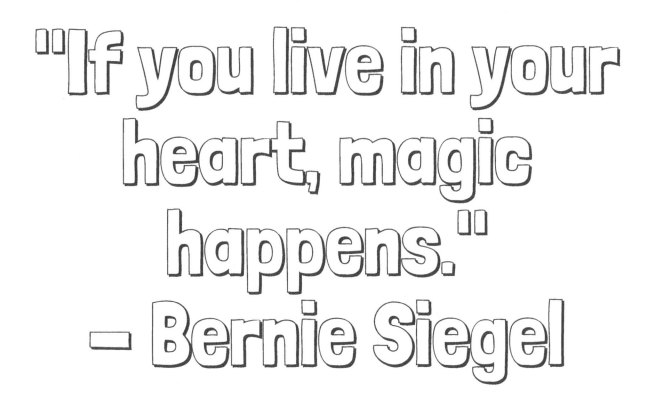

"If you live in your heart, magic happens."
– Bernie Siegel

HOW TO

I created this journal to be completed in the morning AND at night. This will give you the best results. Try it this way first. And then if you feel this is too much and you need to alter a bit based on your schedule that is totally fine. I mean, it is YOUR life after all.

I realize you are a busy gal so each day will start with some good old brain dumps. You know, things you have to get done, how you are feeling, how you slept, etc. Ritual and routine is important in creating healthy habits and becoming aware of the patterns in our lives. When I first did this I noticed that during the full moon I needed an extra hour (at least) of sleep to be of any use to anyone. I wouldn't have noticed that if I wasn't consistent with my tracking and routines.

Each day will have background information, stories, or an educational piece. You can choose to read this before or after you do your morning log. The journaling or daily challenge portion can be completed any time during the day. This is the meat and potatoes. This is where the magic happens. Do this!

You will see colorable quotes + pictures throughout the book. I love using art as creative self expression and to help my right brain come up with creative answers to the journaling prompts. It's also quite relaxing and fun. So doodle or color away!

I am a lover of morning rituals, meditations, affirmations, astrology, creative self expression, and all things self development. These things work… for me. That is why I recommend them. Try them. If you are not feeling it, drop it and pick it up in a few days or weeks. No shame, no blame, no guilt. Do what is right for you.

Lastly, I want to point out that you can read this whole book and do ALL of the journaling in ONE day if you choose to. Then you can come back daily and do your log + review the prompts and contemplate them a bit more.

In appendix 1 you will find information about the moon cycle. Since this is not a dated journal or planner, it is up to you to research the moon sign and phase for each day. A quick google search will do. Or you can download the Deluxe Moon app. #notsponsoredjustafan

Appendix 2 has examples of morning rituals. This comes from my own clients, friends, and family. As with anything, take what you like and leave the rest. I encourage you to go with what feels right. If one day you meditate and the other day you watch Shameless that is totally fine! Just take time for you to connect with YOU.

Appendix 3 is full of affirmations. Choose one, three, or all. Set an alarm on your phone for several times per day. This is your recalibration time. When that alarm goes off, you will say or write your affirmations, feel them, and believe them. This is how we create the person we want to be. And release the person we are not.

"The vast majority of adults have never met themselves."
— Mokokoma Mokhonoana

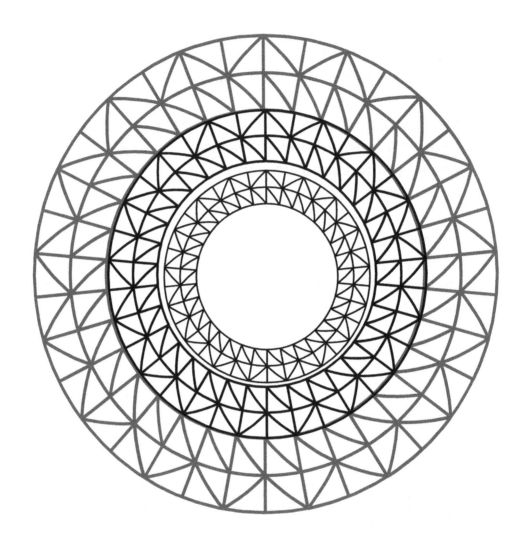

"Be yourself, everyone else is already
taken."
- Oliver Wilde

Day 1

Date:

Moon Phase + Sign:

Meanings:

How did I sleep? Any Dreams?

3 things I want to accomplish today:

5 things I am grateful for:

My recalibration affirmations for today:

AM Ritual:

PM Ritual:

Brain Dump:

Day 1

In preparation for all the magic, it is imperative that we get super clear on what we hope to accomplish here. I gave you my wishes and prayers for you but now YOU need to get clear on what you intend to get out of this for yourself.

Take some time right now to list your intentions below.

WHY do you desire clarity? Why do you desire to find your purpose?

How will your life be different once you find what you are looking for?

How would you feel & what would your life be like if you didn't find this, get clarity, or live your purpose?

Day 2

Date:

Moon Phase + Sign:

Meanings:

How did I sleep? Any Dreams?

3 things I want to accomplish today:

5 things I am grateful for:

My recalibration affirmations for today:

AM Ritual:

PM Ritual:

Brain Dump:

CHAPTER 1:WHO YOU ARE NOT

"Late at night. It all clears away. No distractions. To hide you from yourself." -Earl Hawkins

Day 2

For me, figuring out who I am and what I want meant first analyzing who I was NOT and what I DIDN'T want. It felt appropriate to start here because dissatisfaction is so much easier for us to acknowledge. So, I took a good hard look at what really wasn't working for me.

Take some time right now to evaluate a few key areas of your life to come to terms with what is not working. Brutal honesty is necessary here. If you can't be honest with yourself about what is or isn't working, you are going to have a REALLY hard time accepting your truth & who you are.

Below you will find several life areas. Feel free to add any that are not listed. Please rate each one a scale of 1-10. 1 being super shitty and 10 being magnificent. For any area that you marked less than 10, I want to know what WOULD make it a 10.

For example: if I marked my relationship as a 3, I may note next to it that it could be a 10 if my husband gave me more attention, spent more time with the kids, or if I wasn't married at all. Remember, brutal honesty is the only way to clarity!

This is my approach to goal setting as well.

RATE THE FOLLOWING AREAS FROM 1-10 & BE HONEST ABOUT WHAT WOULD NEED TO CHANGE TO MAKE IT A 10. ((Add categories to the end)

Exercise, fitness, movement:

Friendships:

Romantic Relationships:

Family:

Rest + relaxation:

Stress level:

Physical health (energy, nutrition, weight):

Spirituality/Religion (meditation, mindfulness, sense of higher self):

Career:

Emotional health (moods):

Excitement/fun/overall happiness:

Money:

Day 3

Date:

Moon Phase + Sign:

Meanings:

How did I sleep? Any Dreams?

3 things I want to accomplish today:

5 things I am grateful for:

My recalibration affirmations for today:

AM Ritual:

PM Ritual:

Brain Dump:

Day 3

Today is about getting real with yourself. Whenever we are unsure or confused as children and adults, we tend to ask others for help and advice. But others' opinions are just that, opinions. And they are based on their past experiences and how they perceived those experiences. Few of us actually see things as they truly are, rather we perceive them from our own points of view. Everyone wears their own set of glasses, viewing situations differently and from their own perspective based on their past and the work they have done to heal and understand. So you see, others cannot possibly know what is right or wrong for you because you are so different from anyone else. It's ok to ask for opinions but you must check the information with your own intuition and feelings.

Assuming you haven't done this your entire life and may have taken advice that wasn't right for you, we are going to explore these decisions. Let's look at the category list that you created from yesterday. We will use this as a base.

Why are some scores lower than others? What is going on in these areas? What isn't right? What isn't working? Feel in to what doesn't feel good for you. Is it because you've made decisions based on others opinions? Or maybe you've outgrown this particular situation or person?

Knowing what isn't working is a big clue into what isn't for you. Get real with yourself. This isn't about blame or shame. Explore these areas deeply.

Here is an example from my personal list:

College - I didn't want to go to college but felt I had to. I listened to others as to what I should major in and where I should go. It wasn't right for me. I didn't listen to my intuition and felt others knew better than me about what was right for me. Jobs - I only took certain jobs for money. Eating habits - I developed bad nutrition habits because I wasn't listening to my emotions and feelings. I listened too much to society about what is "healthy". I've learned, and continue to learn that what is healthy for one person may not be healthy for me. Fun - I've lost my connection to fun and don't know how to have fun anymore. This is something I want to explore further in this workbook. What I actually enjoy doing and what fun really looks like for me.

Where have you made decisions based on what others thought?

Exercise, fitness, movement:

Friendships:

Romantic Relationships:

Family:

Rest + relaxation:

Stress level:

Physical health (energy, nutrition, weight):

Spirituality/Religion (meditation, mindfulness, sense of higher self):

Career:

Emotional health (moods):

Excitement/fun/overall happiness:

Money:

"If you want something new, you have to stop doing something old."

- Peter Drucker

☆   ☆   ☆

Day 4

Date:

Moon Phase + Sign:

Meanings:

How did I sleep? Any Dreams?

3 things I want to accomplish today:

5 things I am grateful for:

My recalibration affirmations for today:

AM Ritual:

PM Ritual:

Brain Dump:

Day 4

I'm a tad bit obsessed with the subconscious mind. The subconscious mind is fascinating because it observes EVERYTHING. But the most interesting part is that the subconscious mind absorbs most until about the age of 7. Meaning that your patterns, stories, beliefs, and values were created around that time. And get this, about 85% of the choices and decisions you still make today come from your subconscious mind. Your inner child is still in charge of your life!

Being an immigrant child from Israel at 8 years old, my subconscious mind created the idea that I was different, not good enough, and that no one would love me for who I was. Therefore I needed to change and adapt in order to be accepted and loved. Repetition is key for the subconscious so I affirmed this and was shown it in my reality over and over again with friends, family, boyfriends, etc. Always trying to fit in, I did what others wanted me to do, I said what I thought they wanted to say say, and I started looking how they wanted me to look.

Chances are your story isn't much different than mine. Maybe you didn't immigrate to this country but you have probably spent a good portion of your life doing what others wanted you to do in an effort to be loved, connected, and valued. As humans these are our fundamental needs and wants.

That took you away from the real you. Every time you chose other's opinions over your own, you shifted the energy inside of you away from the real you. This was my AHA moment in life. If I could just de-program, un-condition and go back to who I used to be I would find myself again. If I could only stop myself from trying to fit a square peg into a round hole.

Which is why I've dedicated years (and continue to) to un-condition my subconscious mind and my life in an effort to return to self.

What is the story that you'e been telling yourself? That you're not good enough, that you are not pretty enough? That you are too fat, too skinny? Too old, too young? That no one would love you if you were successful?

What would others think if you got divorced?

The goal for today is to find those subconscious triggers that keep you stuck, playing small, and not living your authentic self.

WARNING: today is journal heavy + life changing!

* What do you believe about yourself?
* What are your own objections to having the things you desire?
* What things do you do that you hate?
* What haven't you told anyone?
* What brings you shame or guilt and how is it still affecting you? <--- this one is SO important.

Shame is a tough wall to break. It pushes us FAR away from our truest selves. But it also shows us our deepest false narratives and beliefs about ourselves. If you feel shame around a memory, you are out of alignment with the truth. Either in terms of values or in terms of reality (you are creating something that isn't there). Do you feel shame because you failed to meet your own values or those of others (which is not your truth)? How do you continue to create similar situations for yourself? Find the pattern!

A common side effect of shame or guilt is feeling unworthy. If you feel not good enough to have, receive, or be, you will continue to create situations of unworthiness in your life. Let's look at the situations that caused you to feel undeserving.

These can be tough. Take your time. Be thorough. Write as if no one is watching (because they're not)

We will be exploring the shadow of the subconscious mind a bit more in the next days. So I want to make a note about trauma. What you have been through should never be compared to anyone else. From abuse to lack of attention, to sexual assault, to bullying. It doesn't matter how small or huge you think it is compared to others'. This is EGO not truth. Accept it, respect it, and get help for it. Don't let you ego tell you it is not important or not BIG enough. Remember, the subconscious mind is a child. She creates all sorts of stories and ideas from her limited understanding. My point is, no matter how big or small you may believe your traumatic experiences may have been, they deserve the time and the healing. Seek out a therapist, coach, or mentor if you need additional help and support.

Notes from Day 4:

_____

_____

_____

_____

_____

_____

_____

_____

_____

_____

_____

_____

_____

_____

_____

_____

_____

_____

_____

_____

_____

_____

_____

Notes from Day 4:

"Shame is how we see ourselves from other people's eyes."
- Brene Brown

Day 5

Date:

Moon Phase + Sign:

Meanings:

How did I sleep? Any Dreams?

3 things I want to accomplish today:

5 things I am grateful for:

My recalibration affirmations for today:

AM Ritual:

PM Ritual:

Brain Dump:

Day 5 is all about the shadow (insert evil laugh here).

What is shadow work? The shadow is TRUTH that used to be in the light. But for some reason (usually traumatic events), it became just a shadow of the truth. Darkness is not bad. We as humans give dark and light labels of good or bad. It just is. It just needs to be accepted as it is and then healed.

Let's take my example of being an immigrant. As a very young child I felt connected and accepted, because I didn't know anything else. This was my truth. Then something happened (moving) that changed this belief and created a shadow within the subconscious that I am not accepted or loved as I am. In doing shadow work, I became aware of this, accepted it, healed it, and brought it back into the light (by no longer acknowledging it as my truth). Doing that stops it from running my life and it stops the subconscious from repeating patterns and making decisions over and over again that come from this shadow belief. Does it remove the shadow all together? Not always. We are paradoxical beings. We will always have both shadow and light within us. We will never be beings of pure light without darkness on this planet (or we would have already ascended past this planet). It is part of our purpose to learn what is dark and light and accept it. And try our best to transmute the darkness that holds us back so that we can live to our highest potential. But it doesn't always happen overnight.

Shame, guilt, fears, judgements, limiting beliefs, shadow stories, all of these lower vibrational frequencies need to be accepted and only then can you truly work through the traumas and un-truths. That means you really have to accept yourself as you are in this moment.

There is always work that needs to be done around shame. So if you feel you want to dive deeper into the shame that you feel, you may do so today. If you feel you have covered the depths of your shame yesterday, we will move on to fear for today.

Fear arises when we feel unsafe, threatened or in danger. Most of the time fear is irrational. Because it comes from the ego. We all have an ego to keep us safe from lions and tigers, burglars and murderers. Fear can be personal and collective. We are energy beings that feel each other consciously and unconsciously. Fear cannot be completely eradicated, it's in our DNA. But if you have the courage to face it, turn toward it, and get intimate with what it wants, you can move past it.

Fear can be irrational, manipulative, and harmful to your psyche. Easily making up and manipulating what could happen. Other times it is based on preconceived notions that are attached to the past. For instance, as a child I learned that when I am myself (super honest and maybe a bit loud) I will not be accepted or loved. Therefore, I developed the fear of being 100% honest with people all the time. It was a conditioning that I had to break through to reconnect to my truest self.

Below are different exercises for squashing fears. Keep in mind that the best, most effective way to really get over (or get through) a fear is to feel it and do it anyway. Cliched but true. Address and clear out your fears. Which ones are real threats and which are just illusions? Sometimes it's the fear of fear that is really driving you nuts.

Exercise 1: List all of your fears and how they are related to trauma, shame, or conditionings. Can you get clear on the specific situations that may have created these fears in order to face it and acknowledge what it is trying to show you? Really explore this and give your fears the space and time to speak to you. Remember, awareness is always the 1st step to healing and growing.

Exercise 2: Play out your fears. Play them out in your head and on the following page. What could happen, how probable is that, what would you do, how would you react, what is the worst case scenario, what is the best case scenario? After every question you can ask yourself "Do I know this to be true 100%?" Meaning, am I sure without a shadow of a doubt that this will happen? Play it all out and then identify for yourself if this fear is a real threat or just an illusion that you've created for yourself?

Notes from Day 5:

Notes from Day 5:

Day 6

Date:

Moon Phase + Sign:

Meanings:

How did I sleep? Any Dreams?

3 things I want to accomplish today:

5 things I am grateful for:

My recalibration affirmations for today:

AM Ritual:

PM Ritual:

Brain Dump:

Day 6

Before we go ahead and let some of this shadowy stuff go and really forgive ourselves, I want to talk about the shit no one likes to talk about. The advantages to having gone through whatever you went through. Here is what has been true for me: the subconscious mind creates certain situations to please us because it thinks we want it on some level and for some reason.

In this instance lets think about the subconscious mind as a 5 year old. Your 5 year old just painted a beautiful picture for you. You don't have the slightest idea what the brown mess is but your child is so proud of himself that he is beaming. He gives you the painting waiting for you to be ecstatic, so you praise him and his masterpiece although inside you are thinking 'wtf?'. Do you see where I am going with this? The child IS your subconscious mind and the picture is your life. Acknowledge the gift, thank the child, show him that you love it because it was created FOR you whether you understand it or not.

Its the same for situations that the subconscious mind creates that we don't consciously want. Take the situation that you are in right now. Perhaps at the crossroads. Not sure which way to go, feeling confused, alone, and scared shitless of the unknown. What are the benefits of this situation? Why would your subconscious mind create this for you?

Here are some reasons I had come up with for this:

My soul knows something is wrong and is trying to push me in the right direction. Chaos creates birth, I am birthing a new me. On a deep level I actually enjoy the search for the real meThe search for the real me keeps me busy, gives me purpose. Maybe I am still trying to find the 'me' that people will like? When I am experimenting, I have less responsibility. I hate responsibility.

Try this now. Choose a shadowy belief, shameful situation, or anything that you may have journaled about in the last few days.

What situations has my subconscious mind created for me?

Why did it create these?

How might this situation be what I wanted? How is it serving me?

What may the advantages be?

Notes from Day 6:

Day 7
_____

Date:
_____

Moon Phase + Sign:
_____
_____

Meanings:
_____
_____

How did I sleep? Any Dreams?
_____
_____
_____
_____

3 things I want to accomplish today:
_____
_____
_____

5 things I am grateful for:
_____
_____
_____
_____
_____

My recalibration affirmations for today:
_____
_____
_____

AM Ritual:
_____
_____

PM Ritual:
_____
_____
_____

Brain Dump:
_____
_____

Day 7

Today is about clearing space and letting go of some of these things that we've been journaling about. Heavy, heavy. If you feel you need another day or two to digest, process, accept, by all means take your time. Just try to continue the daily routines and log sheets.

To some, clearing space means really accepting yourself for where you are today. To others it means forgiving your parents, friends, and yourself for every "wrong" action or decision. The goal is to let go and create space for who we truly are. I have "wrong" in quotes because I don't believe we ever make a wrong decision. It taught you something, it helped you understand, it brought you closer to something. There are always advantages. ((Remember the exercise from yesterday?))

Forgiveness is not about condoning. Forgiveness is about releasing the energy within you and the connection that you may have with a specific person or situation. Forgiveness, to me, means deciding that you want to be free from this and no longer let it leech your energy and consume precious space within. Forgiving doesn't mean you can't be angry. It is not an exercise is spiritual bypassing. It is meant to be used when you are ready to let go. I do not believe in rushing the process but it is absolutely a game changer. And everyone should be ready to forgive at least themselves for one thing or another at this point.

Before I give you my forgiveness exercise I want to talk about surrender. Surrender is about letting things go that are out of our control. Freeing the energy from your body to make space for the things that you CAN control while also allowing God, the Universe, or your higher self to step in and take care of this for you. It's allowing yourself to be in the flow. So before I introduce the meditation, ask yourself this:

If I could lay it all out on the table what would I lay down to surrender?

Then go to www.dannayahav.com/book-extras to download a forgiveness meditation.

Do this each day for the next 7 days (at least) as part of your morning ritual to create space, love, acceptance, and compassion for yourself and others. Creating this space will make room for amazing things come your way.

Notes from the meditation + thoughts about forgiveness:

"When you forgive, you heal. When you let go, you grow" - Anonymous

Day 8

Date:

Moon Phase + Sign:

Meanings:

How did I sleep? Any Dreams?

3 things I want to accomplish today:

5 things I am grateful for:

My recalibration affirmations for today:

AM Ritual:

PM Ritual:

Brain Dump:

Day 8

Look back at the lists you've made the past few days. The things that aren't working, the things you dislike, the shame, the guilt, your fears, your limiting stories, and beliefs about yourself, all of it. The things you forgave and the things you didn't.

Use the rest of this page and the next one to write the opposite of everything on your list.

Re-frame, re-phrase, turn the 'not you' into the REAL you.

You can use these reframes as your daily affirmations .

Examples:

I am not good enough —> I am more than enough

No one would respect me if I quit my job —> I respect myself when I am doing what I truly love in life.

My kids will suffer if I get divorced —> my kids will be happy when I am happy.

I shouldn't have dated that jerk —> He taught me how to love myself

I am ashamed that I don't know who I am and I am 35 years old! I am ashamed that I can't find happiness in the things that I already have —> I have felt lost for a long time. It is ok for me to give myself space and time to find my passions again. I take solace in knowing that my soul knows who I am. I am just learning to listen to her more deeply.

Notes from day 8:

"You are you. Now, isn't that pleasant?"
— Dr. Seuss

Recapping Chapter 1: Who You Are Not

In chapter 1 we got clear on your intentions and what you want to get from this workbook. Remind yourself now what your intentions were from day 1:

We took a look at some key life areas and assessed our level of satisfaction. We also identified what it would take to get a to a 10 in that category. Thus created mini goals for ourselves. Make note of these goals below:

We tackled those things that are NOT you. Those things that are not working and why. Then we spoke about what is holding you back within your subconscious mind such as shame, guilt, fears, limiting beliefs, and old stories. What are the top 3 shadows holding you back right now?

We rephrased and re-framed trying to get to the TRUTH of YOU and your real essence. We also forgave, let go, and released in order to start fresh.
What are your new affirmations that came from reframing your shadows?

Great work! Celebrate yourself!

"Be who you are and say what you feel, because those who mind don't matter, and those who matter don't mind."
— Bernard M. Baruch

CHAPTER 2:WHO YOU ARE

Day 9

In this chapter we will discuss who you already are.

We live in a society where it is hard to choose. Supersize, overload, and overwhelm. So many options, things to try, places to go, foods to eat, subjects to study. Yet we are often pressured to pick just one thing and stick with it. It's so much easier for people if you stay the same. Be an accountant my whole life?! No thanks. We do not need to identify with any consistent identity. Change is good remember? Push away from the idea that other people's comfort should be your priority. It is not. That is their problem. You are allowed to change your mind if you choose.

Who am I, truly?
What is my purpose?
What is right for me, at least for right now?

These are just some of the questions that I would ask myself daily.
We are going to explore all of these in this chapter.

Chances are you have already had some experiences in your life where you were living your authentic truth. When you were just being you and really enjoying it. Those are the experiences that we want to leverage and explore.

Let's start here: make a list of some of the most meaningful times in your life. And why they were magical. What feelings did they elicit?
i.e. - When I backpacked through Europe with my best friend.
When I got married.
Friendsgiving dinners.
Start from your earliest memory and work your way to present time. Make sure to note WHY this was meaningful (friends, family, excitement, adventure, etc.).

Highlight the most important words. Color them in. Re-write them BIGGER. The places you've been, the things you have done, the way you felt, these are all important. They shaped you. These are things you like and enjoy. Perhaps things you even desire MORE of. Can you remember these experiences and begin to really FEEL in to the experience of being authentically you? When you are in joy, in love, in excitement, you are in truth.

FREEDOM   EXPANSION   PASSION   JOY   EXCITEMENT

Day 10

Date:

Moon Phase + Sign:

Meanings:

How did I sleep? Any Dreams?

3 things I want to accomplish today:

5 things I am grateful for:

My recalibration affirmations for today:

AM Ritual:

PM Ritual:

Brain Dump:

Day 10

One of my favorite days. Today we explore the things that LIGHT you up. Those things that set your soul on fire. And also those things that are part of your design... they are inherently YOU whether you like it or not. I'm pretty sure you'll like it too.. as soon as you can let go of what others think ;)

Put your hand on your heart, take several deep breaths, center into your energy and answer the following questions as honestly as you can:

1. What can you spend hours doing? You know when it feels like 15 minutes but you look up and realize it's been 4 hours.

2. What do others often compliment you about? (great listener, so eloquent, gives great advice) - while we don't care what others think ... we are often so hard and judgmental when it comes to ourselves that it may take others noticing our strengths for us to recognize them.

3. What part of your personality have you been shamed for? (being too honest, boy crazy, wild, loud, etc.).

4. What part of yourself have you tried to hide or deny for fear of what others will think or say?

5. What do you deeply desire for yourself or your life? (keep in mind, deep desires can feel shameful. They require vulnerability, courage, and stepping out of your comfort zone.)

6. What are you naturally good at?

Notes from Day 10:

"Imperfection is beauty, madness is genius and it's better to be absolutely ridiculous than absolutely boring."
— Marilyn Monroe

Day 11

Date:

Moon Phase + Sign:

Meanings:

How did I sleep? Any Dreams?

3 things I want to accomplish today:

5 things I am grateful for:

My recalibration affirmations for today:

AM Ritual:

PM Ritual:

Brain Dump:

Day 11

This next exercise is about values and truth. Values are the things that are most important to us, those things that we won't back down for. And yes, these too can change. I do believe we come into life with a set of values from past lives but it is up to us to feel into this lifetime. ((Have you noticed a pattern of FEELING into things yet in this workbook?)) Just as our identities may change several times through life, your values and your truth may grow and evolve too.

The degree to which you can speak your truth and live your truth is the degree to which you are aligned with your higher self. Your higher self is that part of you that knows everything — it's where your intuition speaks from. It's that magic sauce within you that is able to collapse time, see the past, present, and future, give the best advice, and creates miracles (but more on this later). Anything that is not truth, will not feel good, as we saw earlier in this workbook. That is why we worked on clearing the shadows before we spoke about truth. If you are speaking, acting, and living from your shadow, you are not in your authentic truth. So while shadow work tends to last a lifetime, each time you bring the shadow into the consciousness and heal it, you are one step closer to living fully in your higher self energy.

A good way to find your truth is to identify your values and those things that are most important to you. Doing this will give you a clear perspective on who you are.

I always thought that values were something like "do not kill. do not cheat. do not lie." Essentially the 10 commandments. But after doing MUCH research (which I encourage you to do as well), I found values were much more.

Its about your personal truth and what rings true for you. What feels so good you know it must be a part for you? What feels so wrong that the opposite must be right? My values may not be the same as yours. But living in my truth means that I am open and able to respect your values because I stand so firmly in mine. It's crucial to understand that my truth does not have to be yours and this is part of what makes us all different.

My truth is that everything happens for a reason. My truth is that we are all reflections of each other. My truth is that any beef I have with someone else, is only with myself. My truth is that each moment reveals my truth. My values are health, peace of mind, creative self expression, financial security, passion, kindness.

What do you believe in?
What is your truth?
What will make you truly happy?
What could you not live without?
What are your values?

_____
_____
_____
_____
_____
_____
_____
_____
_____
_____
_____
_____
_____
_____
_____
_____
_____
_____

Day 12

Date:

Moon Phase + Sign:

Meanings:

How did I sleep? Any Dreams?

3 things I want to accomplish today:

5 things I am grateful for:

My recalibration affirmations for today:

AM Ritual:

PM Ritual:

Brain Dump:

Day 12

How do you define or describe yourself? Write a short blurb about who you are:

There are many ways to define ourselves. Introvert, extrovert, mother, wife, child, daughter, cheater, liar, beautiful, young, old, fat, ugly. But there is SO much more to you and me than any of these titles or labels. I honestly believe we can create ourselves to be anything that we want, as long as it's what WE want. But I also believe that we are perfect just the way we are. You don't NEED to make yourself into anything else for validation or love. That hardly ever works. You have innate gifts, personality traits, quirks, and weird ass aspects of yourself that make you YOU. Accept yourself for all of it. The good, the great, the ugly. And others will too.

Acceptance = magic

I didn't begin to FULLY accept myself until I learned about Human Design. Now this may sound a bit woo woo but hear me out. I call it astrology on crack. It's your astrological chart + the Chinese I-Ching + Kabbalah + the chakra system. It's a closed mechanical system. There is so much WOO and so much PRACTICALITY to it that it really is mind blowing. Other than giving me a clear understanding of who I was designed to be, Human Design really gave me permission to ACCEPT myself. Including my flaws, because they are divinely mine.

What Human Design couldn't give me, The Gene Keys did. The Gene Keys are similar to Human Design but offer a more fluid, higher frequency understanding of who we are, how to heal our shadows, and to reach our highest potential. The Gene Keys allow you to contemplate, heal, and integrate your shadows and wounds which increases your vibrational frequency unlocking your innate gifts.

Do yourself a favor, download your charts for both. Start with Human Design as it can be more pragmatic and then graduate to the Gene Keys when you feel ready. Search professional readers. Or if you don't want to go that route, there is truly so much you can learn on your own!

Run your Human Design chart here: www.jovianarchive.com. Then head over to interiorcreature.com for additional resources. As for Gene Keys, you can check out teachings.genekeys.com. I also encourage you to join my private Facebook Group: High Vibe Spiritual Tribe where we have studied these topics, shared our charts, and knowledge.

One of the most powerful takeaways from my work in Human Design is that decisions should not be made in the mind. They should be made in the body. This resonated so deeply for me because once I was able to feel into things and get out of my mind, the magic happened. I talk about this a lot (as you have probably already noticed). I am incredibly passionate about this... your body is your BEST tool. It is incredibly intuitive and can reveal loads of secrets about who you are, what you love, hate, desire, and need (more on intuition development in the next chapter).

Today's challenge is to look into your Human Design or Gene Keys chart. If nothing more, just research your type + profile from Human Design (your personality traits).

Notes:

Chapter 2 recap: Who You Are

In chapter 2 we focused on your past joyful experiences. Who you were in those memories, what you loved, and how you felt. These experiences were important because feeling good and joyful means that you were standing in your truth. That you were aligned with your true self. We want MORE experiences like that. Make a list below of those experiences or feelings that you felt:

Passions + desires! What are you passionate about? What do you desire? Write some key words below from this exercise on day 10.

We talked about values, truth, Human Design, and the Gene Keys. Phew. We did some soul digging in this chapter. I hope that this chapter gave you some clarity into who you ARE. What are your biggest takeaways from everything that you have learned in this chapter?

Day 13

Date:

Moon Phase + Sign:

Meanings:

How did I sleep? Any Dreams?

3 things I want to accomplish today:

5 things I am grateful for:

My recalibration affirmations for today:

AM Ritual:

PM Ritual:

Brain Dump:

CHAPTER 3: YOU ALREADY KNOW

Day 13

We already have the answers that we seek inside of us. I believe that we come to this planet to play with, heal, and even struggle with certain energies. Have you ever noticed how certain things are easy for you? Like you've already mastered them?Jealousy… not a big deal for me. I've done some work around it and now I feel perfectly fine when others have things that I want. I know that it's the Universe telling me I can have it too if I do the work. This is an energy that I have already worked with and healed. Other energies are not as easy for me. How do I know what I need to work on? It's inside of me. My intuition will always guide me towards those things that I am meant to work on, those things I am meant to be teaching, learning, and experiencing. All I have to do is be still, trust, listen, obey. We will cover these aspects of intuition development plus several others in this chapter.

Intuition development is a huge stepping stone to getting to know your truest, most authentic self. Your intuition is the language of your higher self. It is there for you to use and to align to the energies that will create miracles for you, lead you to your purpose, help you find passion, and guide you towards the amazing life you were meant to live.

Believe it or not, you have actually spent the last 12 days tuning in to your intuition. If you let your answers flow from within you and you've worked on your shadow, you've been listening and using your intuition. See, it IS that easy.

Intuition is a calling, it's a sign, it's a whisper, it's a feeling, it's a knowing. And it is always happening in the present moment.

Place your hand on your heart. And write down the FIRST word that comes to mind for the following questions.

What do I need right now?

What do I know to be true about me?

Where am I not listening but should be?

What is most important for me to know at this moment?

The way that intuition works is that when it tells you what to do, you should do it. Every time that you don't, and you ignore it instead, the whisper becomes weaker. The more you trust and the more that you follow, the louder and stronger it becomes leading you toward miracles and magic.

Can you remember a time that you followed your intuition? What happened?

What about a time that you didn't follow it? What happened then?

Day 14
_____

Date:
_____

Moon Phase + Sign:
_____
_____

Meanings:
_____
_____

How did I sleep? Any Dreams?
_____
_____
_____

3 things I want to accomplish today:
_____
_____

5 things I am grateful for:
_____
_____
_____
_____

My recalibration affirmations for today:
_____
_____

AM Ritual:
_____
_____

PM Ritual:
_____
_____

Brain Dump:
_____
_____

Day 14

Your body follows the soul. Your body is an antennae for energy and information. Who you are today, who you are meant to be, what you are destined to experience... these are all within your soul. Your soul knows what's right for you. And it speaks to you through your intuition. Humans spend most of our time thinking the same limiting thoughts pretty much all day long. We get so stuck inside our heads and we create these elaborate stories based in fear. Because of that your intuition will often get your attention through the path of least resistance, the body. Aches, pains, gut feelings, chills, disease... these are all intuitive hits from your soul telling you something is wrong. Showing you who you are and whether you are on the best path for you.

Today is about silence, stillness, and getting intimate with your body.

Spend more time in your body, today. Being completely still. Asking your body for answers and listening until you can feel it rise from deep within. If you've never done this before, keep in mind it may take you some time to get comfortable with this exercise and really trust what comes through. You will need to get your ego and mind out of the way. The ego will tell you this is ridiculous and that you have so much to do and don't have time for this shit. But don't give up. Not now. Remember the pain and struggle you feel when you are lost and confused? Let that pain be so much worse than forcing your mind to shut up.

Learning how to communicate with your body and decipher its messages is important because it will help you better understand intuitive hits and also yourself! If you know that when your stomach feels tight it means that you are acting from fear, you will be more conscious to explore it next time. If you know that when your throat gets tight, you are holding back truth, you'll be more vigilant next time it occurs to speak up. The body has so much to teach you about yourself. You just have to tune in.

I've created a meditation for you to help you get into your body. You can find it here: www.dannayahav.com/book-extras or google to find one that you love.

Write about your experiences or insights on the next page.

Day 15

Date:

Moon Phase + Sign:

Meanings:

How did I sleep? Any Dreams?

3 things I want to accomplish today:

5 things I am grateful for:

My recalibration affirmations for today:

AM Ritual:

PM Ritual:

Brain Dump:

Day 15

We often think life is linear. That everything should happen a very specific way. Preferably a way that doesn't freak the ego out and makes perfect sense, logically. Well guess what, honey bunny? That has not been my experience at all. Especially when it comes to intuition.

As I said earlier, your intuition will speak to you through the path of least resistance. Wherever and whenever you are not in control is how your intuitive hits will come. So if you are able to successfully sit in meditation for 20 minutes each day clearing your mind, you may find that your intuition will speak to you during meditation. However, how many of us can actually do that? I can't fully do it everyday yet!

So your intuition will go elsewhere. Your body. That's why it's important to talk to your body. But your intuition will also show you things, let you hear things, and bring you things that are outside of yourself. They are in your environment. Yup, I'm talking about "signs from the Universe".

But these are actually signs from yourself, from your intuition. Begging you to pay attention, get curious, and get moving if things are not working out where you currently are.

Today's challenge is to set an intention or ask a question. Then to look for the signs, messages, overheard conversations, FB posts, Instagram pics, e-mails, bus posters, or anything else that shows up. Something will show up to answer your question. You just have to be aware and present.

One of the questions I ask (a lot) is, what is my next phase? What should I be focusing on or studying next? Several months ago, I asked and then sort of forgot about it. I went on Instagram and followed a rabbit hole of hashtags, user accounts, and then a podcast. It was Human Design. I got in my car to listen to it and as I was driving the car in front of me had the license plate: 8888889. I obviously googled this and while I found a lot of different definitions, this one resonated deeply: "your life purpose is fully supported by the Universe." For me this was a message that I needed to keep learning about Human Design and that it would provide me with many answers (which it has!) If you follow me no Instagram (@this.is.danna) you'll notice that I post repeating number pics in my stories, a lot. That's how I often receive messages from my intuition!

The lesson? Follow your intuition, don't try to control, don't expect things to happen in logical ways, be open, be aware, be curious, explore. Have fun!
Write about your experiences and signs from today.

Day 16

Date:

Moon Phase + Sign:

Meanings:

How did I sleep? Any Dreams?

3 things I want to accomplish today:

5 things I am grateful for:

My recalibration affirmations for today:

AM Ritual:

PM Ritual:

Brain Dump:

Day 16

What is your purpose? What is anyone's purpose? Is it a job? A state of being? A feeling? The Gene Keys' Richard Rudd explains that we are each born with a gift. And our purpose is to express that gift (or energy) in ourselves and out into the world. Living out your full potential IS your purpose. Living, learning, serving, growing, and healing through the energies you were born with and those accumulated in your life is your purpose. I believe that our purpose is ever changing as are we.

If my gift is that of helping others discover themselves and live their purpose, I can do that in multiple ways. I can do it through coaching, through courses, through books, events, or even by letting others watch me do it for myself. I have found Human Design and Gene Keys to be able to convey what energies I am meant to play with in this lifetime extremely well. The Gene Keys' activation sequence provided SO much clarity for me on my gifts, higher spiritual purpose, and life's work. So you can refer back to your charts from chapter 2 to take a closer look at the energies within you.

We've touched on many different aspects of a person's purpose. Still, here are a couple more Qs to help you dig deeper for more clarity.

What are you most curious about right now? Curiosity = Intuition.

Who would you be if you knew you couldn't fail?

Look backwards to move forward. Your past will show you your patterns + shadow and most likely your mission and purpose in life as well. Your experiences and the way they made you feel will help clarify your values and those things that are important to you. Dealing with incredible stress and health issues in my life has led me to really value good health, nutrition, sleep, exercise, and self care. I value my body and its magic and teach this to all of my clients as well. It's a value and part of my purpose. What past events have shaped your purpose or mission in life?

Additional Notes from Day 16:

Chapter 3 recap: You Already Know

In this chapter we learned that we already have all of the answers inside of us. We just need to develop our intuition, listen to it, and then obey. Trust is another element of the process. You must trust yourself and the information that you receive. This comes from trial and error and experimentation. I hope you experimented with listening to your intuition, your body, seeing signs, and becoming aware of the information that is all around you and within you.

Lastly we talked about purpose and mission.

Take some of the key words from day 16 + some of the key words from day 13 + the ones from your chapter 1 and 2 recap pages and write them below. Create a mission statement for yourself based on what excites you, what you're curious about, what your desires are, what you love, and what you've learned about yourself.

Create your purpose. And be open to how it may change yearly, monthly, or even moment to moment.

My personal mission as of now:

"I lead, inspire, and teach by being authentically ME."

"The great spiritual geniuses, whether it was Moses, Buddha, Plato, Socrates, Jesus, or Emerson... have taught man to look within himself to find God."
-Ernest Holmes

Day 17

Date:

Moon Phase + Sign:

Meanings:

How did I sleep? Any Dreams?

3 things I want to accomplish today:

5 things I am grateful for:

My recalibration affirmations for today:

AM Ritual:

PM Ritual:

Brain Dump:

CHAPTER 4: WHO DO YOU WANT TO BE?

Day 17

Think back to when you were about 10 years old. Who did you want to be back then? What did you want to be when you grew up?

Research shows we know ourselves at the highest level around that age. Now of course, this will also depend on the type of upbringing and childhood that you had. So if you feel certain events in your childhood may have flavored your goals negatively, we can take this line of questioning in a different direction.

If you had an empty slate right now (meaning you were a kid again), what would your goals be for the future? What would you want to achieve? What would you want to have? What are the experiences that you would want to have? Who are the people you would want to meet?

You can write this from the perspective of your 10 year old inner child or from the perspective of an adult with all the possibilities and potentials in front of her.

Not knowing much about the world and perhaps still having your innocence in tact, what did you believe you were capable of? Can you latch on to that child's hope and dreams? Ride the wave and explore how some of these elements are still true today? Perhaps you still want to be a writer (or blogger). Maybe you would still love a cooking show (or to cook for friends).

Additional Notes from Day 17:

Day 18

Date:

Moon Phase + Sign:

Meanings:

How did I sleep? Any Dreams?

3 things I want to accomplish today:

5 things I am grateful for:

My recalibration affirmations for today:

AM Ritual:

PM Ritual:

Brain Dump:

Day 18

Allow yourself to dream really BIG.

And write it all down, often.

Writing is a great way to affirm to your subconscious mind that THIS is something that I want to experience. An amazing medical intuitive that I worked with once asked me, "If I gave you the choice of a Lamborghini or a horse & buggy to drive across the country with, which would you choose?" The horse & buggy is the same as speaking your affirmations out loud. While the Lamborghini is compared to WRITING your affirmations, dreams, and goals." So you see, there is real power in putting the pen to the paper.

The best way I have found for really engaging the subconscious mind and the conscious mind in creating the person I want to be (and the life I desire to live) is by scripting my dream life and day.

Set the mood for this one. Light some candles, incense, and get a mimosa. Whatever makes you feel lush, alive, excited. Now script your perfect day. Starting with when you wake up in the morning. What do you wake up to? Is there a man next to you? Maybe sex? Maybe you wake up to the sounds of the ocean? How do the sheets feel? What do you smell? Who is beside you? What does he/she look like? What do you smell like? How do they touch you? How do you touch them? DETAIL is key. After waking up do you sit for meditation, do yoga, walk around the block with your beloved, read a book? The more details you can sink into this and the more you can feel from it the better.

Please allow yourself to dream as big as possible. There is no fear. This is a perfect world scenario. You can have anything you desire.

A note about MONEY. Money is energy, just like everything else in life. If you wrote money then I want to know WHY you want the money. What will the money give you? Freedom? Peace of mind? Luxuries? How will you feel with all the money in the world? What will you do with it and why? What feelings do 'boat loads of cash' elicit?

Script your perfect day:

_____

_____

_____

_____

_____

_____

_____

_____

_____

_____

_____

_____

_____

_____

_____

_____

_____

_____

_____

_____

_____

Once you have completed your ideal day, re-read it, and feel it all over again. Highlight or underline some KEY aspects that really speak to you. (i.e. - living by the water, having a morning routine, being a hairdresser, etc.) things that make you smile and say ooh-ahh.

"Follow your inner moonlight; don't hide the madness."
— Allen Ginsberg

Day 19

Date:

Moon Phase + Sign:

Meanings:

How did I sleep? Any Dreams?

3 things I want to accomplish today:

5 things I am grateful for:

My recalibration affirmations for today:

AM Ritual:

PM Ritual:

Brain Dump:

Day 19

We are going to continue the momentum of the last 2 days by focusing on the person that we want to be. In this challenge today, we are going to meditate and meet our future self. This is a guided meditation available for your at www.dannayahav.com/book-extras.

Before you begin the meditation write a few questions below that you would like to ask your future self.
Here are some examples:

- How did I start my business?
- Did I have another child?
- What is the process I took to find my purpose?
- What does my purpose look like?
- Am I happy? What did I do that brought me the most happiness?

This works in giving you new information when you are completely relaxed, when you throw caution to the wind, when you don't try to control, when you trust what you hear (see or feel). Practice, practice, practice. If you find it easier to journal instead of meditating, you can absolutely do that. Listen to the prompts and journal your answers.

Why does this work? Your higher self (where your intuition comes from) is not linear. Space and time do not exist. Therefore, your higher self is able to know the past, present, and future as if it is all happening at the same time. And it may be, if you believe in parallel realities, but that's for another book. So when you are able to access your future self (or higher self) you are able to tap into her well of knowledge and understanding in an effort to retrieve information in the present. Because it's all happening now!

Give it a shot! Write your questions below.

Meditation or journaling notes from day 19.

Recapping chapter 4: Who Do You Want To Be? In this chapter we explored your goals from childhood, your dreams and hopes, your perfect day, and meditated on HOW you go to the future you desire.

Summarize your findings from the chapter below:

What do you desire for yourself?

Which life standards are non-negotiable for you? What are you prepared to work and fight for?

How do these dreams and goals relate to those you wrote about in Chapter 1, Day 2?

"Always be a first rate version of yourself and not a second rate version of someone else."
— Judy Garland

Day 20

Date:

Moon Phase + Sign:

Meanings:

How did I sleep? Any Dreams?

3 things I want to accomplish today:

5 things I am grateful for:

My recalibration affirmations for today:

AM Ritual:

PM Ritual:

Brain Dump:

CHAPTER 5: BE HERE NOW

Day 20

Before we dive in I want to take a second to really honor you and commend you on the work that you've done thus far. It's been almost 3 weeks which means you have probably successfully changed some habits and re-wired some neural pathways. You are certainly on your way to a transformed life. You are an inspiration to women everywhere and to me. I heart you and would love to hear from you. Send me an Insta message today and tell me how it's going (@highvibespiritualtribe).

The purpose of chapter 5 is to really ground everything that we have been exploring. I want you to unpack it and figure out how you can start implementing the important things into your life. It's really great to know who you are and feel it on a deep level but if you're not acting it or living it, well what's the point?

Today we will chat about speaking up for what you want. There is this "joke" within the coaching community. Something to the affect of… "there are so many broke coaches out there because no one is actually asking for the sale, the client, the money."
That's just it, princess, you have to ask for what you want! This is the number one rule in manifestation as well. ASK and you shall receive.

Today's challenge is to get super brave and ask for some of the things that you've discovered that you desire. Ask for the raise, ask for the divorce, ask for the job, ask for some space to just BE. Have uncomfortable conversations, if they are necessary. Do the things that you must do right now to set up a strong foundation for you to be you, unapologetically. I heard a prominent coach say recently that the best way to determine how successful you will be (or are) is by the amount of uncomfortable conversations you are willing to have. It's true. Not only in terms of success. But also in terms of self confidence. The more you stand up for your values, desires, purpose, and mission, the more confidence you will have in just being you.

I want to make a note here: While I give you full permission to be you as fuck and have those difficult conversations about what you desire, I also want to give you permission to take your time making big decisions. Huge, life changing decisions take care, compassion, and transparency. I believe in divine timing and I believe you will know when the time is right to do what you need to do.

What difficult conversations do you need to have? Where can you speak your truth? What do you need to ask for?

You can't be committed to your bullshit + your growth. It's one or the other

Day 21

Date:

Moon Phase + Sign:

Meanings:

How did I sleep? Any Dreams?

3 things I want to accomplish today:

5 things I am grateful for:

My recalibration affirmations for today:

AM Ritual:

PM Ritual:

Brain Dump:

Day 21

Creative self expression is just that: the way that you creatively express yourself. This can be in terms of the clothes that you wear, the tattoos on your body, the way you do your hair, your hobbies, and the way you live your life.

I want to discuss one specific way of expressing yourself and who you are: the way you look. I know I know this doesn't sound spiritual at all and you shouldn't judge a book by its cover and blah blah blah. But here's the thing. I don't give a fuck what others think of the way you look and neither should you. This is all about what makes you feel amazing and like yourself.

For instance, I love tattoos. I really do. It's the way I've been expressing my journey. Every milestone documented on me. My parents don't love it. Some friends are against it. Even my husband doesn't love all of them. But it's me. And they are mine. And they are my way of expressing myself that make me feel good in my skin. The clothes I wear are me. The way I do my makeup (or lack therefore) is me. When I let my hair be crazy wavy and a little frizzy it's just me. My point is, if others don't like it, they can bounce. There are 7 billion other people on this planet!

Today's activity is to discover the things that make you, well, you. And do them. Do you LOVE wearing heels but feel silly? Do it anyway! You'll get over that feeling of silliness when you focus on how great it makes you feel. Do you feel fabulous when your hair is straight? Straighten it once a week but then also feel into your natural waves. How can you accentuate them? How can you accept your naturalness?

Try not to spend time criticizing yourself but focus on the way you are and why that's beautiful. Also focus on the things you do that maybe others don't like. The clothes you love that your husband doesn't. Practice just being you and expressing who you are through your clothes, through your body, through your looks. Focus on putting the REAL you out into the world.

P.S. - If you are having trouble with this, try an impromptu dance party first. TRUST ME!

What worked? What didn't? How did you feel?

Day 22

Date:

Moon Phase + Sign:

Meanings:

How did I sleep? Any Dreams?

3 things I want to accomplish today:

5 things I am grateful for:

My recalibration affirmations for today:

AM Ritual:

PM Ritual:

Brain Dump:

Day 22

Let's refer back to the recapping of chapter 4. Remember that great list you made of ALL the important desires, feelings, dreams, goals, passions, and values?
Choose your top 5. Maybe it's from your mission statement. Whatever feels most authentically you, write it here now. How would you describe your TRUEST self?

How can you LIVE this list daily?

What can you do to elicit these feelings every single day?

What can you do to be more yourself in each moment?

For example, if you picked freedom as one of your values or desires, you may find that yoga makes you feel free and open.

If health is a value and priority for you you may find that taking your vitamins while reciting and affirmation or blessing your 8 glasses of water a day is a ritual you connect deeply with.

Try to put an action on each word you chose to describe the real you.

Here are some ideas:
- speak your truth
- dance
- yoga
- meditation
- explore a new desire each week
- travel (or plan travel)
- explore Pinterest for interests
- create a vision board
- work out
- eat healthy
- read
- have mind blowing sex

The key here is to act, be, feel your authentic self more than NOT. I realize this may take time. I mean think about it, you have spent 30, 40, or even 50 years acting, deciding, and thinking the way others want you to. So yes, it takes time to decondition and recondition back to your authentic self. That is why it is so necessary for you to feel the feelings of being you and act the way you want to act, even in tiny ways...daily!

Day 23

Date:

Moon Phase + Sign:

Meanings:

How did I sleep? Any Dreams?

3 things I want to accomplish today:

5 things I am grateful for:

My recalibration affirmations for today:

AM Ritual:

PM Ritual:

Brain Dump:

Day 23

Pinterest. I love Pinterest for their secret boards while I am trying to figure out what I like, love, or dislike this month. I have boards for my "values", for 'art", for "things that are so me", for my "bucket list". Use this tool to search for colors that you love, prayers that resonate, outfits you want to wear, people you wish you could see, things you want to do before you die, things you want to try, foods you want to eat. This is really a free for all allowing you the creativity and privacy you need as you explore your innermost passions and ideas. So allow yourself the freedom and excitement to search, pin, revisit, and feel all the feelings for these things as though they are already here, already inside of you... because they are. Your curiosity IS your intuition telling you... "hey girl this is part of who you really are.. explore this". Allow yourself to do just that.

One of my amazing clients took this project and gave it her own spin. She created her own "mix tape" on Spotify with songs that resonated for her. I urge you to get creative and do what feels right for you.

Bucket lists are really good for getting your CRAZY desires and ideas down without really having the PUSH to do any of it right away. But it is saved somewhere with your energy behind it so your subconscious mind knows to bring this to you so that you can experience it, at some point. Why I love bucket lists is because whenever I look at mine I immediately feel at home in my heart"YES, this is me. THIS is what I really want to do and experience. These are my goals and dreams." I urge you to have crazy ass things on your bucket list but also things that seem achievable in the short term. Like hot yoga, camping, visiting a random state on a normal Monday. Then, make it a point to do one of these "normalish" bucket list things once a week or once a month. Call it AUTHENTIC YOU time.

Takeaways:

Day 24

Date:

Moon Phase + Sign:

Meanings:

How did I sleep? Any Dreams?

3 things I want to accomplish today:

5 things I am grateful for:

My recalibration affirmations for today:

AM Ritual:

PM Ritual:

Brain Dump:

Day 24

I don't like my clients to compare themselves to others so I want you to understand this is NOT about comparison. This is inspiration. Throw yourself into the rabbit hole of FB or Instagram (my personal favorite) and check out what other people are doing, how they are living, what they are eating or drinking, what they are reading or saying. Keep in mind that social media is simply the highlight reel. The way people look on social media is hardly ever the truth. But, you can absolutely gain some inspiration from others in this way.

For instance, I follow @christina_sutra. I don't compare or judge but I really admire her vulnerability. I admire her truth speaking and being who she is no matter what others think. So I allow this sort of energy that radiates from her to influence my own life and my work. I know that I crave more vulnerability in my life. Which is why I am so inspired and turned on by her. Find people that turn you on and light you up.

Make notes below on who inspires you and WHY you admire or find inspiration from them. Remember, everything is a hint for what you love, desire, and who you are. Explore!

Here are some of my faves from Instagram: @christina_sutra @synergysoul @iampaigemichelle @valeriemesa @sophie.jaffe @this.is.danna (me, obvi), @nicholesylvester, @undefinedthemag (also me :))

What did you find?
Who did you find?
Why are you intrigued?
What might your intuition be telling you that you need more of in your life based on this?

Chapter 5 recap: Be Here Now

In chapter 5 we put some action behind our journaling. We focused on living our truth, dressing authentically, being proud of how we look, staying inspired and motivated, and also creating a safe place to store all of our authenticity.

We also set the foundation for our truest selves by having some deep and perhaps uncomfortable conversations with others. Great job!

What actions can you commit to taking that will help you live your authentic self daily?

"There is no competition among wild women. They are too wild to be caught in a tiny space of envy. Instead, they dance together & allow the good to flow abundantly to them"
- Anonymous from Instagram

"SUCCESS IS 80% MINDSET AND 20% MECHANICS"
- TONY ROBBINS

Day 25

Date:

Moon Phase + Sign:

Meanings:

How did I sleep? Any Dreams?

3 things I want to accomplish today:

5 things I am grateful for:

My recalibration affirmations for today:

AM Ritual:

PM Ritual:

Brain Dump:

CHAPTER 6:
LOOKING FORWARD

Chapter 6: Looking Forward

Here is what we will cover in this chapter: metaphysical transformation in a practical manner. Yep, it's all connected.

Daily mindset work (air-mental), support (water - emotional), soul work (fire - spiritual), and physical nourishment (earth), relationships (ether), and a special self love/care bonus.

Before we get started on mindset, I want you to define success. What does success mean to you and how will you know when you achieve it? $100K in the bank? Daily dinners with the family? Working your dream job? Waking up happy and excited every day? Do this first.

Day 25
Air: mental.

This is about your thoughts. This is NOT spiritual bypassing. I don't want you affirming away your shadows. You already know how to work through them. This is about maintenance.

Remember, when we discussed the subconscious mind and how it makes decisions for you based on past patterns and beliefs? Repetition is how you break that. So while you have been crushing some limitations the past few weeks and working on clearing the shadows, everyone has set backs and that's ok. It's not about the setback or the failure it's about how quickly you rebound. By the way, I don't believe in failures, everything is just a lesson and an opportunity to learn and course correct where something didn't work.

Since repetition is key, I have found that listening to daily podcasts, YouTube videos, and specific Facebook lives has really helped teach me more about my subjects of interest but also inspire and motivate me to kick ass every single day. I encourage you to find some of your own podcasts to follow or videos to watch that will provide you with that extra jolt of motivation.

Listen, you have spent the past 30-50 years being conditioned one way. Now that we are undoing that, it's going to take some time and some work. But don't give up. Consistency is super important. Even if it's not perfect (there is no such thing as perfect by the way). Just be consistent with whatever mindset work you choose to do. Reading, listening, watching, journaling.

Limit the things that don't make you feel good. Watching the news first thing in the morning, reading the paper before bed, trashy TV shows, scary movies. Pay attention to what affects you and limit it. We want to feel good, be good, do good.

What can you commit to doing daily to build a mindset of steel?

Day 26

Date:

Moon Phase + Sign:

Meanings:

How did I sleep? Any Dreams?

3 things I want to accomplish today:

5 things I am grateful for:

My recalibration affirmations for today:

AM Ritual:

PM Ritual:

Brain Dump:

Day 26
Water: emotional.

When you feel tired, rest, don't quit. It's normal to feel overwhelmed when doing this work. Trust me, I've been there and sometimes breaks are a necessity.

Through all the work that we have done, have you been able to identify when your are about to have a 'down in the dumps' day? You know, one of those days where you can't work on you anymore and just feel like eating a pint of ice cream curled up on the couch in the fetal position? ((Never had one of those? Yeah, me either ;)))

Are you able to listen to your body and just give it what it needs (maybe rest)?

What are the common emotions that arise for you when you are feeling down or low? Get to know these, notice them, and figure out WHY they are showing up. What are they trying to communicate to you? What do they want? Remember, your body is always sending you messages.

There is a lot of great work that you can do on your own. And I absolutely recommend that you do some of this work on your own. But I have to admit to you that my life began to truly change once I hired a powerful, high level coach. Someone to call me out on my bullshit, stop me from playing small, and to ask the deep questions that pulled out all the old crap I didn't even know was there.

I encourage you to find a great coach, a therapist, someone you trust, and a tribe. People that will listen intently and let you be who you are. Speaking your wounds is transformational alone. Think about it, you are finally EXPRESSING any repressed feelings that have become depressed!

Today's challenge is to find that coach and your tribe. I have my own tribe on Facebook: High Vibe Spiritual Tribe, and I would love for you to join. But, there are millions of other groups on Facebook too. I also encourage you to find a local support group or spiritual/religious center around you that you feel comfortable with. Try MeetUp.com.

As humans we are meant to feel connected and be connected. Remember Human Design? Human Design shows you how your energies intertwine and connect with others'. How your energy affects other people and how they affect you. So while it is super fun to do this work alone on your couch with a bottle of wine, get out there! Meet some peeps, get some support, join a group, find your tribe, learn something new!

Did you find a coach/mentor? Did you find a tribe/group?

Notes from today:

Day 27

Date:

Moon Phase + Sign:

Meanings:

How did I sleep? Any Dreams?

3 things I want to accomplish today:

5 things I am grateful for:

My recalibration affirmations for today:

AM Ritual:

PM Ritual:

Brain Dump:

Day 27
Fire: Spiritual.

We are multifaceted beings. We are not just our minds or bodies. We have this soul inside of us that is burning for some action, passion, and excitement. Several days ago we spoke about the things that light you up. Those things that you could do for hours without realizing that time has flown by.

Think about your soul as being in your heart. When your heart expands or beats widely. When you feel warm all over and alive. That is the soul being LIT UP. Clearing out some shadows, fears, and old beliefs, it gives your soul a chance to shine, to be heard, to glow, to be free.

I know you've done a lot of work on the shadow but I also know there are some things you are avoiding doing the work on. What are they? It's usually the first thing that comes to mind. ((dig deeper if you need to, no one is watching))

Why are you avoiding these things? What are you afraid of? What will happen once they have cleared out? How do they STILL benefit you?

Fill your free time with healing and nurturing. Give your soul the time of day to speak its wounds. As you would a child, nurture it and support it. And let it shine. What are the things that you have found that really light you up? That make you come alive? That help you express yourself creatively? That help your soul feel seen, heard, and nourished? Art? Yoga? Reading? Cooking? Dancing? How does your soul love to express herself? Remember your list from day 22? Refine it and put it into action.

For me it's reading. I love spending time reading and that really feeds my soul. It's also part of the self care that I require (more on that later). I also love yoga for my soul expression. After a good 60 minute hot flow class I feel as though I have given my soul time to speak and breathe. I feel alive and free.

Notes:

Day 28

Date:

Moon Phase + Sign:

Meanings:

How did I sleep? Any Dreams?

3 things I want to accomplish today:

5 things I am grateful for:

My recalibration affirmations for today:

AM Ritual:

PM Ritual:

Brain Dump:

Day 28
Earth: Physical.

Have you learned yet that everything is connected? That everything is energy? Including the things that you put into your body and mind. As we learned earlier, your body is an antenna for energy and information. It is how your higher self communicates with you many times. If you are filling your body with processed shit, chemical laden foods, and low vibrational drinks it will affect the way that your body can receive information. It just does. There's a lot of research out there saying that your gut is a brain. The health of your gut affects your mental and emotional states. I believe it. Everything is connected.

Where can you clean up your diet? Remember you know the answers. You don't HAVE to look outside of yourself. Chances are you already know! Just be honest. What do you have to do to have a cleaner body that is more attuned to energy? If you had previously pulled your Gene Keys chart, take a look at your radiance sphere.

Remember to listen to your body. What may be a "healthy food" may not be for you. We are all wired just a bit differently. If gluten doesn't work for you then it doesn't. And you'll know because you'll feel like crap, be bloated, and feel foggy. If you listen, or even document the foods you are eating and how you are feeling you will learn SO MUCH about yourself and your body. I encourage you to do this as it will only increase your intuition and you'll feel so fresh in the mind, body, and soul.

Start small but start somewhere. Your inner state will reflect in your environment. Add in veggies, take out the soda, limit the sweets, drink more water. Small consistent steps to success.

Document your foods from today + how they made you feel:

Day 29

Date:

Moon Phase + Sign:

Meanings:

How did I sleep? Any Dreams?

3 things I want to accomplish today:

5 things I am grateful for:

My recalibration affirmations for today:

AM Ritual:

PM Ritual:

Brain Dump:

Day 29
Ether: Relationships.

As you increase your personal frequency (by doing this work) you will notice that things begin to change in your life. Maybe some are good and some are bad. People will be triggered and you may also. Some friends may leave your life creating space for new ones to come in. Your husband may judge the work or mock it. But remember, it's about how YOU feel. We are all different. We are all meant to do different work. What feels right for one person may not feel right for another. This is what makes you uniquely you. This is what finding yourself and living in alignment with your authentic self means. It means having the courage to do what's right for you.

Look at the changes in your life as shifting energies. As the energy (happiness, satisfaction, fun) increases in your life so does your personal energy. You are constantly creating your reality. So when you change your frequency you are going to be creating a reality that is on a different frequency. And some of the old people or things may no longer be a vibrational match to you. Learning to let go is important. It's hard but it's often necessary. Remember, letting go just means you are creating space for the new. Listen to your body and how it feels.

While some people will bounce out of your life others will trigger the fuck out of you. What this means is that they will say and do things that elicit an emotional response from you that may make you a bit nutty. Take a step back and ask yourself these questions.

What is it in this person that triggers me? Label them, label it.
Is this something that is also inside of me? When was the last time I behaved this way? Have I dealt with that situation? Cleared it out?
Is this something I wish was inside of me? Am I jealous or envious?
Is this something that I recognize and HATE inside of myself? Ahem… more work to do here.

You see, princess, it's never about the other person. It's always about you. The subconscious mind thinks the world revolves around you. And maybe it does, since you are the creator of your world. If you are triggered by something, it is often a reflection of yourself that you see in someone else. Work on clearing out triggers, meeting people where they are, and showing compassion for others that don't understand this process.

Work through your triggers below:

What is it in this person that triggers me? Label them, label it.
Is this something that is also inside of me? When was the last time I behaved this way? Have I dealt with that situation? Cleared it out?
Is this something I wish was inside of me? Am I jealous or envious?
Is this something that I recognize and HATE inside of myself? Ahem… more work to do here.

Day 30

Date:

Moon Phase + Sign:

Meanings:

How did I sleep? Any Dreams?

3 things I want to accomplish today:

5 things I am grateful for:

My recalibration affirmations for today:

AM Ritual:

PM Ritual:

Brain Dump:

Day 30

This is one of the most important topics in the entire book. So why did I leave it for last? I wanted you to experience it for yourself before I talked about it.

Self care and self love. People ask me all the time how to increase their confidence and self love. How can I love myself more? And the answer is by accepting yourself and taking care of you. We have spent the last 29 days accepting ourselves for who we are, who we were, and who we want to be. This is the work that creates more love, compassion, and joy. Can you feel it?

What if I told you that without you there would be nothing? That you are the ultimate creator? That you deserve to be treated like the queen that you are? <— all of this is true. Your energy is your purpose. The way you treat yourself reflects in the way you treat others. In the energy you have to give out. When you are compassionate towards yourself you reflect that out and show it to others. Think about it.

Ladies, you cannot fill others' cups from an empty cup. I don't know how this became a THING but you do not need to give, give, and give and leave nothing for yourself. For fuck's sake it is NOT selfish to give a shit about yourself! Yes, I'm passionate about this. You deserve to take good care of yourself. In fact you need to. How can you possibly fulfill your purpose on this planet if you are depleted emotionally, energetically, and physically? You just can't!

I know you've learned something about good self care the past few weeks of doing this work. What is it? The good and the bad.

Have you realized you NEED alone time daily? I do. Or else I can't function. It's like sleep and water to me.

What self care habits can you adopt daily or weekly? Don't confuse self care with self indulgence. Watching a rom com and downing a bottle of wine may be acceptable once in a while but not daily. This is self indulgence and perhaps even addiction (seek help for the latter). Make a list of 25 self care/self love activities for yourself. Refer back to this daily if you can!

Here are some of my personal faves. Write yours below as well.

Meditation
Reading
Coffee outside
Baths
Cooking for myself
Yoga
Prayer
Rituals

Chapter 6 recap: Looking Forward.

In chapter 6 we focused on some metaphysical healing on the physical plane.
Air: mental: mindset
Water: emotional: support
Fire: spiritual: soul work
Earth: physical: nourishment
Ether: relationships: triggers
SELF CARE + SELF LOVE

What changes are you committed to creating after this chapter?
What can you add in to your schedule? What can you remove?
Why do you want to do any of this shit? - The reason many of us don't stick to
commitments is because we don't actually want to do them. Even if someone said once
on Oprah that you should wake up at 5, but if you don't want to, then don't do it!
What DO you want to do?

"Don't you ever let a soul in the world tell you that you can't be exactly who you are."

— Lady Gaga

Bonus Day 31

OMG. It's our last day. Let's circle back to days 1 + 2. What were your initial intentions? Have they been met? Why or why not?

RATE THE FOLLOWING AREAS FROM 1-10 AS OF TODAY & BE HONEST AGAIN ABOUT WHAT WOULD NEED TO CHANGE TO MAKE IT A 10

Exercise, fitness, movement

Friendships

Romantic Relationships

Family

Rest + relaxation

Stress level

Physical health (energy, nutrition, weight)

Spirituality/Religion (meditation, mindfulness, sense of higher self)

Career

Emotional health (moods)

Excitement/fun/overall happiness

Money

Compare this list to Day 2.

What has changed? How has this work affected you? Celebrate yourself for how far you have come. Gloat, be proud, scream it from the rooftops, share with your mentor or tribe!

Feel into it. Feel into the magic that occurs when you are just being you. Feel into the experience of being yourself. How does that feel? How has your confidence and self love improved? What else can you accomplish from this state of being? The world is your oyster. You can have, be, do anything. As long as you are being YOU.

Conclusion

Welp, while I wish I could stay with you forever, the time has come to say goodbye. The show is over. At least this show. If you've enjoyed this 31 day journey, I encourage you to come join me and some other awesome gals in my Facebook group: The Conscious Creators' Club. I also encourage you to reach out should you have questions, comments, feedback, or need additional support in any way. I am also pretty busy over @this.is.danna on Instagram if you wanna come stalk me.

You, my friend, still have some digging, healing, and living to do. How do I know that? Because I do too. I haven't reached my potential just yet and I am still coming across plenty of triggers, old beliefs, fears, and other shadows for me to work through and clear. Some of this work is daunting and long. But, I have been shown that it is worth it and I hold on to that belief as my truth. I hope you do the same.

I hope that this workbook has provided you with a permission slip to be yourself no matter what. I hope it has helped you identify some areas where you hold yourself back. I pray that it has awoken you to your potential and to your strengths and gifts. That it has helped you better understand your purpose and your mission even for just one moment. I hope that it has helped increase your confidence in being who you are and taught you how to flourish in your own skin. Mostly I pray that you have felt seen, heard, understood and that you received the clarity that you have been seeking.

Until next time,

Xoxo

Danna

"The Universe reveals its secrets to those who dare follow their hearts"

APPENDIX 1: CYCLICAL LIVING + MOON CYCYLES

Whether you realize this or not EVERYTHING in life comes and goes in cycles. And I mean everything: the moon, the seasons, creation, manifestation, menstrual cycles, growth, death, days, weeks, months, etc, etc. Energy cannot be destroyed. It flows in and out and on different vibrations and frequencies in cycles and phases.

Let me give you an example: when you wake up in the morning, you may be feeling groggy and tired. As you have your coffee and do your morning stretches, you start to liven up a bit. Going to work you feel ready to conquer the day and be as productive as possible. Around 3 or 4 you start to feel your energy drain and maybe go for a walk or have a snack which provides some more energy. By the end of the day you are tired and ready for sleep. Can you see the cycles?This is a super simplified version of the phases we go through daily, weekly, monthly, yearly.

Think about your menstrual cycle. There are certain things you crave at certain times in your cycle. Emotions that arise and energy levels that change with your estrogen level. And then there's your estrogen level in general that increases, peaks, and then decreases during the course of the month.

So why is this important and why should you care? Being aware of the cycles of everyday life gives you permission to slow down as well as rev up. It helps you be more in sync with nature and the natural flow of the Universe. Become aware of where you are at each point in time and realize that trying to do MORE in a time of rest will only stress your system and have the opposite affect of what you are trying to accomplish. Follow the natural rhythm.

The cycles of the moon have proven to influence us emotionally, physically, and mentally. Think about it, the moon is powerful enough to influence the ocean. And we are 80% water... so of course it will have some sort of affect on us as well.

On the next page is a quick and dirty chart to help you better understand the basic cycles and how they may affect your mood and productivity. After the chart I have included explanations of each cycle as well as activities should you choose to manifest or create something with the moon either during the 31 days or anytime after. The astrology portion is beyond the scope of this book. If you choose to add this to your daily log, you can google or download the Deluxe Moon app.

"The moon is a loyal companion.
It never leaves. It's always there, watching, steadfast, knowing us in our
light and dark moments, changing forever just as we do. Every day it's a
different version of itself. Sometimes weak and wan, sometimes strong and full
of light. The moon understands what it means to be human. Uncertain.
Alone. Cratered by imperfections."
— Tahereh Mafi, Shatter Me

WAXING = moon's illumination is growing
WANING = moon's illumination is decreasing
CRESCENT = less than half of moon is illuminated
GIBBOUS = more than half is illuminated
QUARTER = exactly half is illuminated

New moon: Sun + moon are in alignment. New beginnings, clean slate. Fertility. Fresh start.

Waxing crescent moon: Set intentions, dream, and create goals + vision boards

First quarter: Decision making. take action —push forward no matter what.

Waxing gibbous: Struggle may arise. Refine your goals. Use "failure" as feedback to course correct if needed.

Full moon: Assess your results + accomplishments. Release all that no longer serves including any disappointments from NOT manifesting your desires quite yet.

Waning gibbous: Introspect. Check with your values + beliefs, are you aligned? Be grateful. Allow yourself to release even more.

Last quarter: Be gentle with yourself + nurture. Continue to release anything that is not for your highest good. Struggle may arise.Forgive yourself + others.

Waning crescent: Surrender, rest, reconnect, recommit, have faith… go back to your WHY.

New Moon, who dis?

As we do with every new moon, now is the time to think about goals, dreams, and inspirations. What is it that you truly want to achieve this lunar cycle?

This is the day that the moon and sun are in alignment. As such, it is also a time for you to be in alignment with what it is that lights you up fully in your life. Discover your purpose, let yourself dream big, enjoy day dreams, and imaginary strategy sessions.

In this first phase of the lunar cycle we are spending time acknowledging our desires but also BEING with spirit and with our authentic selves. You see, there are phases to creation as well as to the moon. This first phase of CREATION (because we are all meant to be creators) begins with LISTENING.

For extra points:

- Spend 5-10 minutes just listening without any intentions or purpose other than to just sit in silence.
- Create a list of 5 new ideas that really light you up.
- Go through each one and FEEL into your body.
- Which FEELS the best and most exciting right now?

I want to be clear that you are NOT setting an intention yet but exploring the energy of your desires + dreams. You are spending time with spirit and with yourself just BEING.

This first phase lasts only about a day or so and then we move into the waxing crescent phase of the lunar cycle. THIS is when we will set intentions.

Waxing Crescent

The first part of any creation process is to listen (which we covered with the new moon). This is where the inspiration comes in, the idea forms in your mind. Technically your soul receives it first but it is in the listening, the resting period that you are able to hear this idea and conceptualize it. Although this next moon phase is that of the waxing crescent, we are still in the chill phase of creation.

My exercise for you for the next few days is to be present with the energy of the things you want to create. So if you didn't do the new moon exercise above, now is a good time.

Once you have completed that, it's time to DREAM really big! Do some online research, get on Pinterest, look up inspiration on Instagram (find me at @this.is.danna), listen to podcasts, watch videos. Find the people that have accomplished everything you want, been to the places you want to go, and have the things that you desire. Find the things that INSPIRE you. That REALLY light you up and fill your veins with passion and excitement. Find those things. Either work them into one of the 5 ideas you had above or just create a vision board with them to be achieved at a later date. But the point of this is to make sure each one of those five ideas really lights a fire in your belly!

And if you want to take this one step forward head on over to www.dannayahav.com/book-extras to watch a video on creating a vision board for your smartphone.

Choose one. What is your intention for this cycle? What will you create?

First Quarter

The energy behind the first quarter phase of the moon is all about action.

But don't worry, we'll start small. For your moon activity today, make a list of 5-10 action steps that you can take to get you even one inch closer to your goal or intention for this moon cycle.

Here's an example. My intention is to spend more time being fully mindful and present. So some action steps that are achievable for me are:

1. Spend 5 minutes in complete silence each day noticing the energy around me.
2. Sit down to eat breakfast without a book, phone, computer, tv, or even the kids.
3. Catch myself multitasking at least once a day and STOP it.

That's it! Easy peasy.

But here's where people tend to fall off: take your actionable steps, and actually DO THEM. Decide what you want. Take action. And push forward no matter what. No matter what.

Waxing Gibbous

As the moon's light increases so do our desires, feelings, and emotions. Have you felt as though the clearer you get on your intentions the more you are asked "are you sure"? This can look like you creating situations that are close to what you want but not quite.

That's the energy of the waxing gibbous. It urges us to get super clear on what it is that we are working on, what our expectations are, by when, and what would it actually look like when we achieve it.

Struggle may arise (or maybe it already has) in terms of your intention or goal. Use this as a time to refine your goals, get even more clear on what you want or don't want.

Look at failure as a means for course correction. It's a roadblock that you need to go through. Don't make it a huge deal, just re-route.

Feel at peace with whatever is coming up for you at this time. It's normal, it's right, and all is well.

Full Moon

The natural energy of the full moon is this: assess your results + accomplishments. Release anything that no longer serves you on this particular journey (aka lunar cycle). Also release disappointments and any attachments to outcomes that you have about your manifestations.

Let's create a ceremony around this 2nd fresh start by acknowledging what you want to release and what you want to fill its place with.

Get a piece of paper and make two columns.
Column 1: I'm sorry, I forgive you, thank you, I love you.
Column 2: I AM
Column 1 is everything you want to release and let go of (i.e.- doubts, fears, ex-boyfriends, shame, body weight, haters, etc.)
Column 2 will be the opposite of column 1 (i.e. - I am confident, I am courageous, I am love, I am beautiful, I am healthy, I am a leader, I am happy, etc.)

On or around the night of the full moon, create a sacred space for yourself. Light a candle, meditate, say a prayer. Rip your paper in two separate columns. Then cut apart each of the things that you want to release. As you let each one burn in a fire repeat the Ho'oponopono prayer: "I am sorry, I forgive you, thank you, I love you" and let that baby burn. Inhale deeply and then exhale with force. Repeat for all the other things you are releasing. At the end, read your I AM affirmations at least 3 times through while standing, with force, and with conviction. Remember, when God said let there be light... he didn't whisper it or asked nicely. He commanded it.

Command what you want. Enjoy the light.

Here is the meaning that I attribute to the Ho'oponopono prayer. I am sorry that I let this person, emotion, situation control me. I also take responsibility for any negativity I may have contributed to this. I forgive you for taking up space within me. I forgive you for any hurt you caused. I thank you for the lesson you taught me. I love you for everything that you are and because you are a part of me. We are one. And I let it go. Feel the release.

Waning Gibbous

Waning gibbous means that the moon is more than half illuminated and is now decreasing in illumination as we move away from the full moon and closer to the new moon.

This portion of the lunar cycle is about checking in with your values + beliefs to recognize where you are aligned and where you are not. The intentions that you set during the new moon and waning crescent phase, do they still feel aligned with who you are and what you want? Are the physical manifestations that you are seeing in your life at this moment aligned with your personal value system? Does this assessment phase feel good or inauthentic? Reflect.

Allow yourself to release further this week anything that does not feel aligned. But as you do that don't forget to also be grateful for everything that you have created thus far in this lunar cycle and in your life in general. Remember, you are a creator experiencing your own reality at all times. You created this. Acknowledge that, be grateful for it all, and then graciously release anything that no longer serves you as you become more and more your authentic soul self.

We have about a week to enjoy this introspection and to create further alignment between your true soul self and your reality.

Since the energy of this phase brought about introspection and checking in with ourselves about whether we are living authentically, transparently, honestly, or not; today's activity is about values.

If you have not created your values yet from chapter 2, day 11, go back and do that for the activity of this lunar phase. If you have done it, take this time to look at your values again, evaluate, make changes, or additions.

Last Quarter

It's the last quarter of the moon cycle which means your motivation may be waning just like the moon's light. Take today to be really gentle with yourself. Allow yourself to feel all the feelings without quickly trying to push them away.

Nurture yourself with a green juice, smoothie, huge salad, or something else full of nutrients and love for your physical body. Nurture your mind with motivational videos or books. Nurture your soul with friends, laughing, a coaching session with me :), or a white light meditation.

Continue to work with and release the things that are not serving you. Be honest with yourself and what is not working. This is the time when struggle may arise (which is why we are working on nurturing) but another great exercise is forgiveness. Can you forgive yourself and others? Try a daily practice of journaling, a meditation, chanting, praying, etc. Again, be easy on yourself. Let your intuition guide you as to where you need more nurturing. It doesn't have to happen in one day. Just holding the intention that you would like to forgive or love yourself more is powerful. Small steps.

What are some nourishment activities you can participate in?

Waning Crescent

The last phase of the lunar cycle is the waning crescent.

The waning crescent takes us back to the chillin' phase of the creation process. We started with just being and letting the inspiration download with the new moon and have come full circle now in the last resting phase with the waning crescent.

This is a time to rest and reconnect. Surrender to the powers that be, to the energy that is around you. Don't fight against this energy that may seem heavy and low. Roll with it. Have faith, recommit to your WHY (why you started this journey, what it is that you want, and why). This energy may seem to linger until next week. Probably until the new moon. Many people fight the energy of the waning crescent and try to push harder, do more, fight their body's messages to chill, and end up falling flat on their faces. This phase is not meant for action. It is meant for contemplation, further nourishment, listening, being, and focusing on self care.

How can you spend more time just BEING during this phase?

"There is nothing more rare, nor more beautiful, than a woman being unapologetically herself; comfortable in her perfect imperfection. To me, that is the true essence of beauty."

— Steve Maraboli, Unapologetically You: Reflections on Life and the Human Experience

APPENDIX 2: MORNING RITUALS

Below are examples of morning rituals and practices from friends and clients. This is just meant for inspiration and ideas. Never comparison.

-Wake up at 5:30 AM
-Oil pull for 15 minutes
-Record my dreams, write down what I am grateful for
-Diffuse and apply essential oils
- Drink a lot of water
-Incense, light a candle, pull card(s), meditate, pray
-Stretch and use foam roller
- Listen to something motivational while making my family breakfast
-After breakfast is over I look at my list for the day.
I try not to look at my phone until it is time to listen to my daily motivation.
-Laura Rock, President, Rock Family Foundation.

Wake up at 4:44
Name 5 things I am grateful for before getting out of bed
Speak my affirmations on the way to the bathroom
Read outside for 15 minutes, light incense, say prayers
Journal for 15 minutes
Look at my phone, answer emails + start my day
- Danna Yahav

Up at 4:30am to exercise
Shower, get dressed
Make a cup of hot tea
Out the door
- Maren Osher

When I have the kids... I hit the snooze button repeatedly while I
say my protections and fallback asleep then I run around like a
maniac getting the kids ready ;)
When I don't have the kids:
6 AM wake up
6-6:30 pray/meditate/protections
6:30-7:30 run/walk/give gratitude
- JLM

Drink warm water with lemon
Take my probiotics
Stretch my body while repeating my prayers and affirmations
If I have time to meditate I will, if not I will get ready for the day
-Anonymous

Coffee. Just coffee. But in silence.
-Maria

After brushing my teeth, I get on my yoga mat for some quick sun salutations
and then meditate for 10-20 minutes.
-LD

Mornings are the only time I can work on my side hustle. So I work for an hour and then listen to a podcast as I get ready.

-Jill

Get out of bed on the "right foot"

-Drink plain hot water to refresh and feel good

-Be grateful. For all I am, have, see, and hope to be. Say in my head what I feel grateful for, for that day.

-Put my hand on my heart and feel the warmth.

-Take a few deep breaths and get into my heart. Try to see that warm, flowery space. Connect with it.

-Clean myself from negativity with the violet flame. See it on my, in me, breathe it...

-Ask for protection from Archangel Michael, his ray, and his light. See it around myself.

-Connect to my I AM presence. My higher self. All of the good I ever was... together in a bright light. See that connection in my crown.

-Ask for permission from my family's I AM presence to share the violet flame with them. Allowing them to take from it what they need.. see their goodness and let go of anything not helping guide them and feel love.

-Ask for their protection

-Ask for the permission of the Earth's highest self to use the violet flame to release from negativity from us and know we are grateful.

-Ask for the permission of the I AM presences-of the spirit around me to feel the violet flame, drink it, taste it, touch it, whatever they're ready for-to help them move forward and see their goodness

-SEL

Let yourself be the person you have secretly always wanted to be

APPENDIX 3: AFFIRMATIONS

I AM WORTHY
I AM ENOUGH
I AM WILD + FREE
I AM A DIVINE BEING
I BELIEVE IN MYSELF
I HAVE EVERYTHING I NEED
MY TALENTS ARE BOUNTIFUL
I AM ME AND THAT IS ENOUGH
I AM THE CREATOR OF MY LIFE
MY GIFTS ARE NOW EXPANDING
I AM MEANT TO FOLLOW MY HEART
I HAVE THE STRENGTH TO SUCCEED
I AM BEING GUIDED BY LOVING SPIRIT
IT IS SAFE TO BE AUTHENTICALLY ME
I AM CLEAR IN MY VISION OF MYSELF
I AM CAPABLE OF WONDROUS THINGS
I ACCEPT MYSELF AS I AM IN THIS MOMENT
MY LIFE IS UNFOLDING IN PERFECT TIMING
I CREATE MAGIC WHEN I AM JUST BEING ME
I AM ALWAYS SUPPORTED BY THE UNIVERSE
I HONOR MY SOUL BY FOLLOWING MY HEART
I AM LIVING MY PURPOSE WHEN I AM BEING MYSELF
MY LIFE IS JUST BEGINNING + THE FUTURE IS BRIGHT
MY LIFE IS EXPLODING WITH JOY, PASSION, + EXCITEMENT
I ACCEPT THAT THERE CANNOT BE LIGHT WITHOUT DARKNESS

ABOUT...

The author ...
Danna Yahav is an intuitive life coach, author, and founder of Undefined the Magazine (@undefinedthemag). She is a 1/3 Manifesting Generator, Scorpio sun, Sagittarius rising, and Aries moon.

A true Scorpio shadow worker, she is obsessed with the inner workings of the human psyche and a scrambled egg-hashbrown-sauerkraut concoction. She helps women (and some men) find, accept, and worship themselves fully.

She is a lifelong learner and has been studying metaphysics, spiritual development, and mindset work for over 10 years. She uses an extensive array of tools from many different modalities to help women have incredible breakthroughs and transformations in their lives. When Danna isn't creating content, coaching, or writing she enjoys spending time with her two children Zeve & Maya and their many friends and family members.

Staying in touch ...
You can find Danna in her free Facebook group: The Conscious Creators' Club
On Instagram @this.is.danna
Online at www.dannayahav.com where I create new blog posts, courses, freebies, masterclasses, challenges, and more!
Don't forget to download your free meditations + extra goodies for this workbook at www.dannayahav.com/book-extras

"Do your own thing on your own terms and get what you came here for"
— *Oliver James*

NOTES

Made in the USA
Monee, IL
02 November 2020